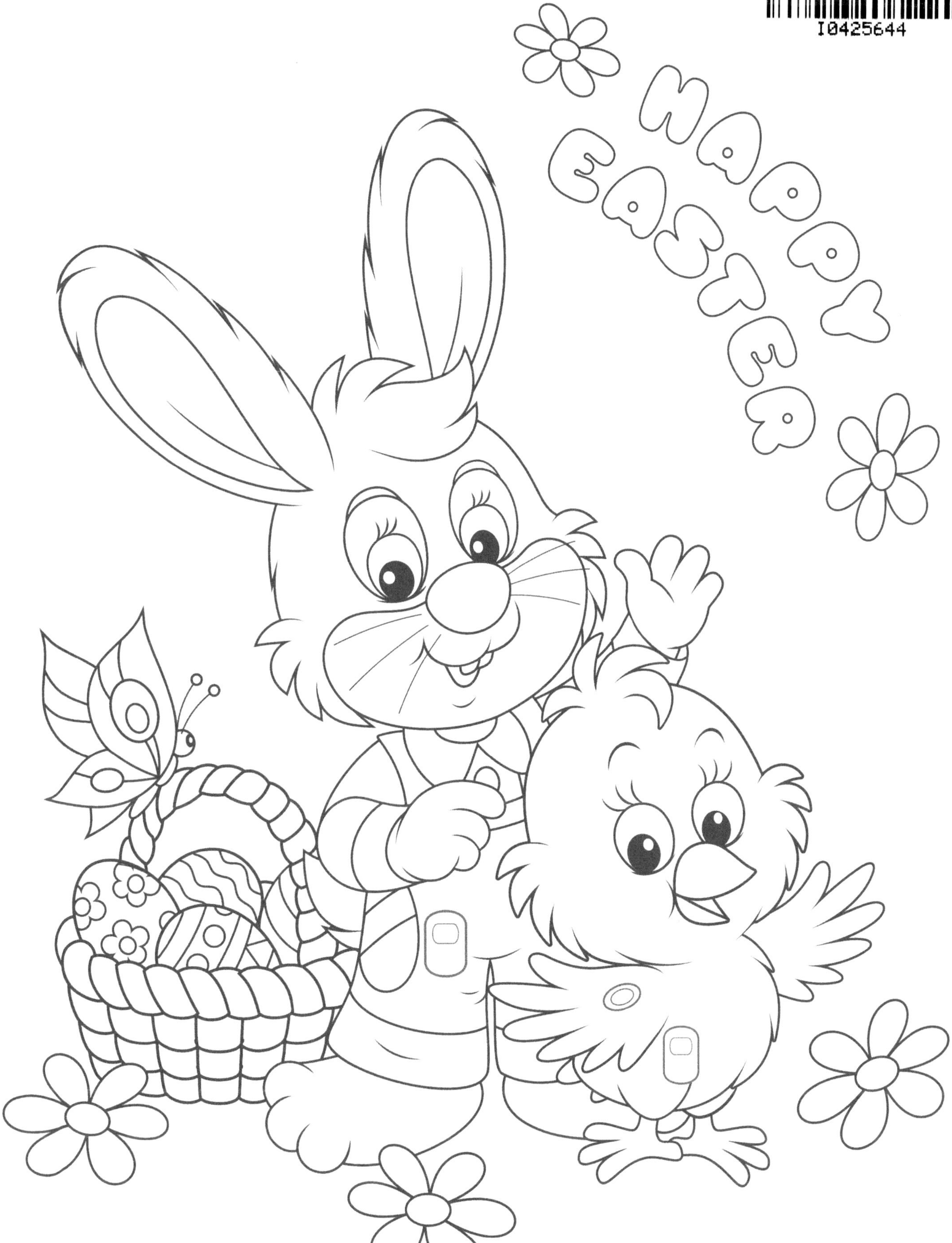
HAPPY
EASTER

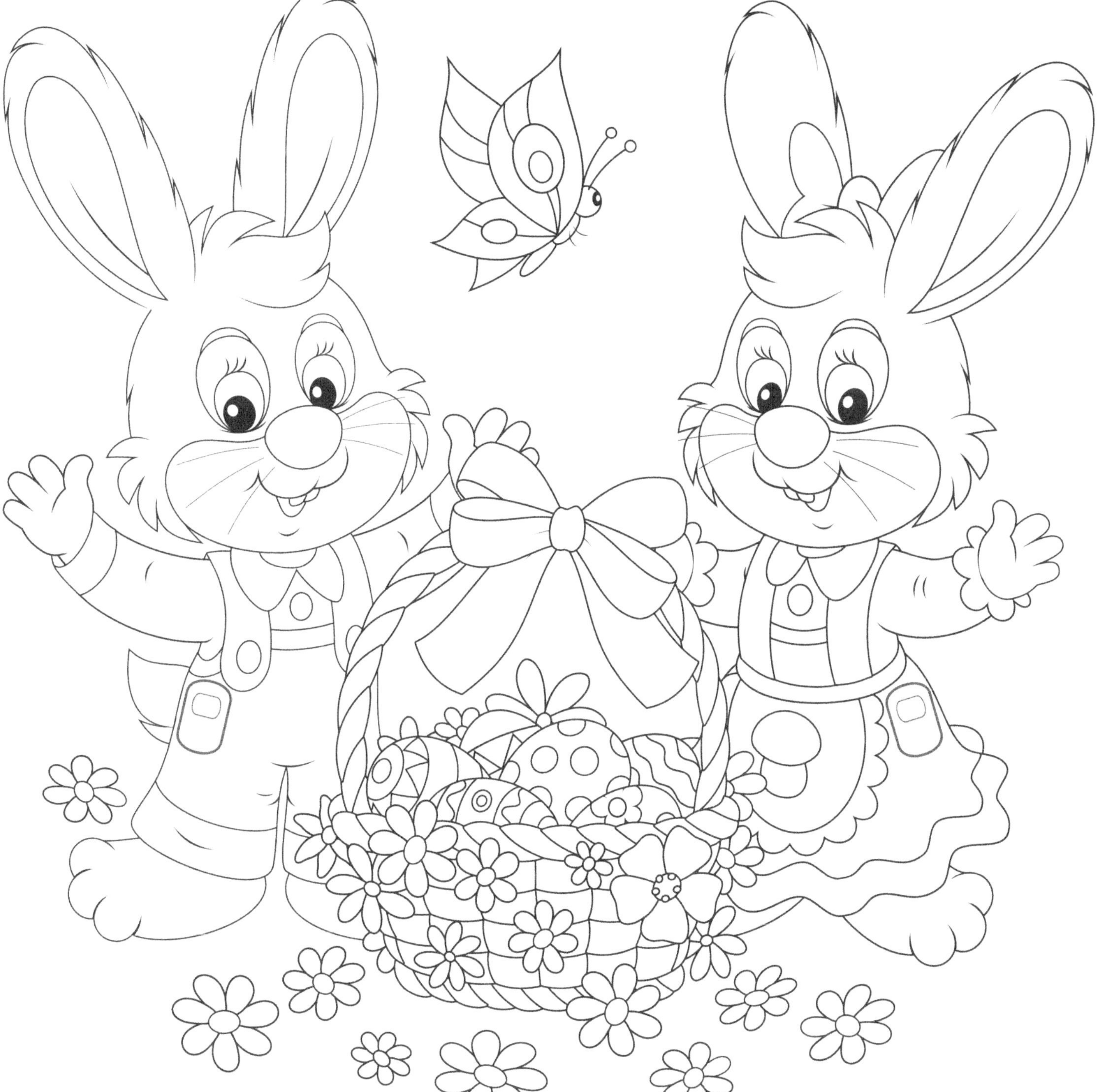

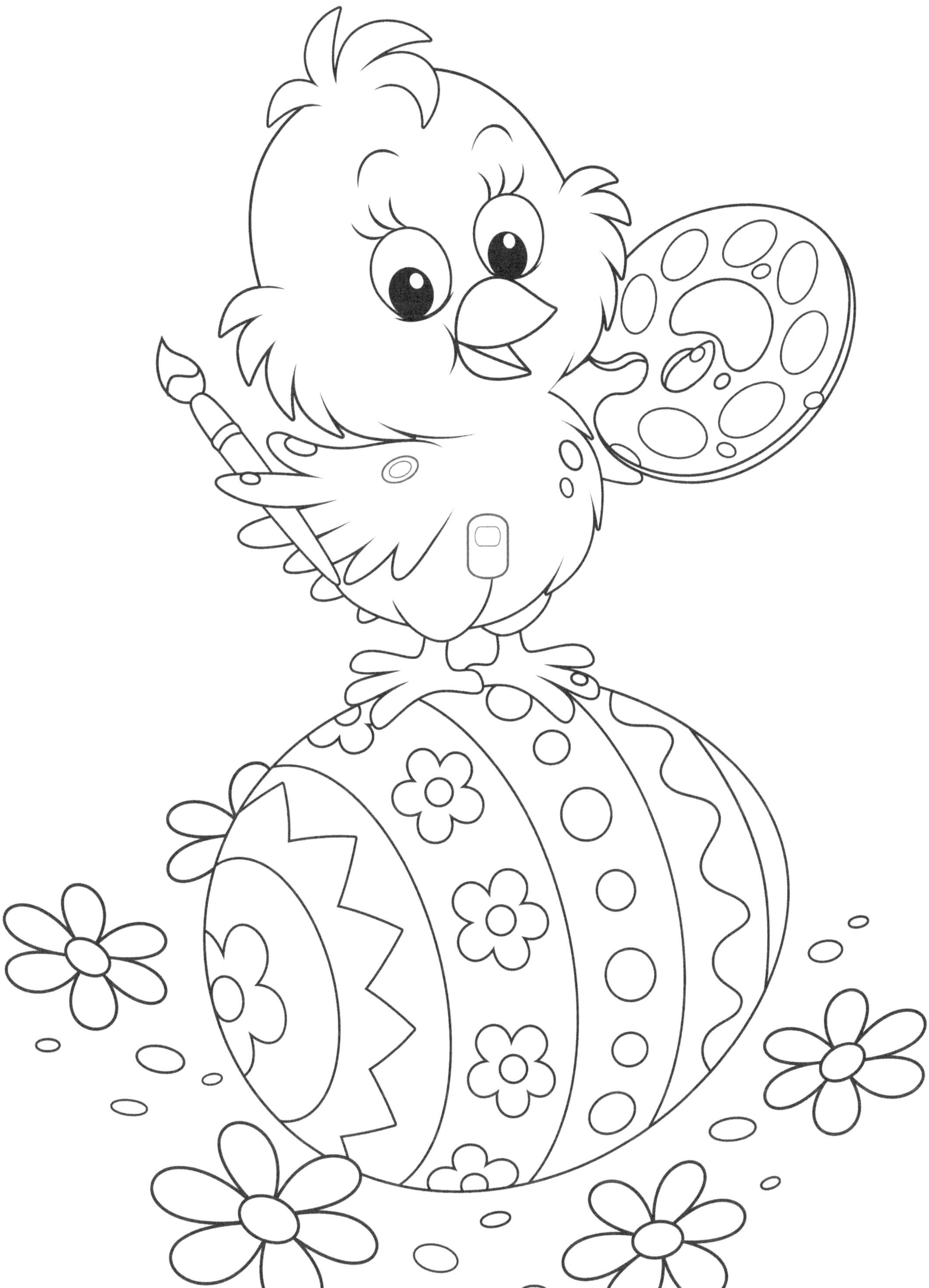

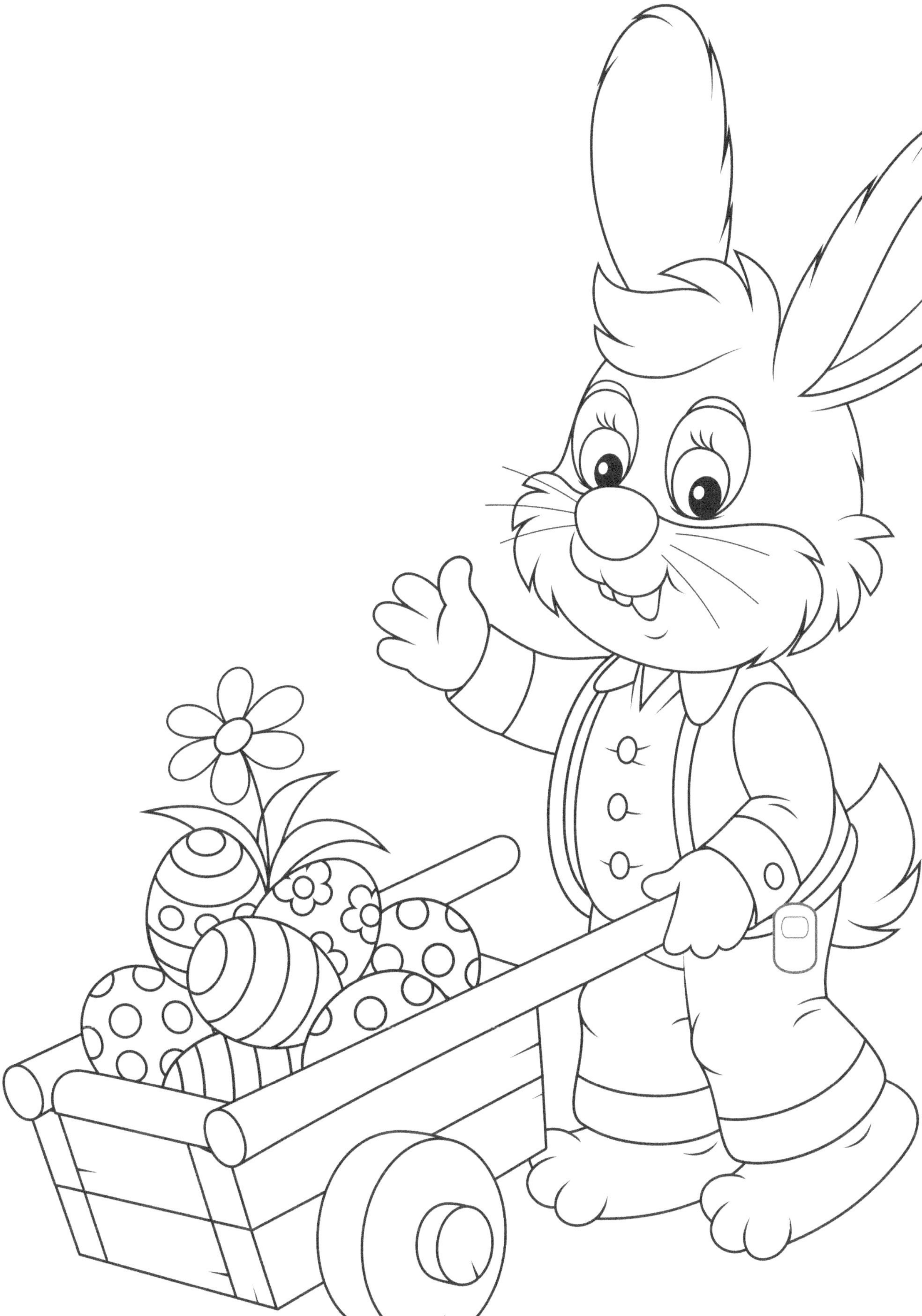

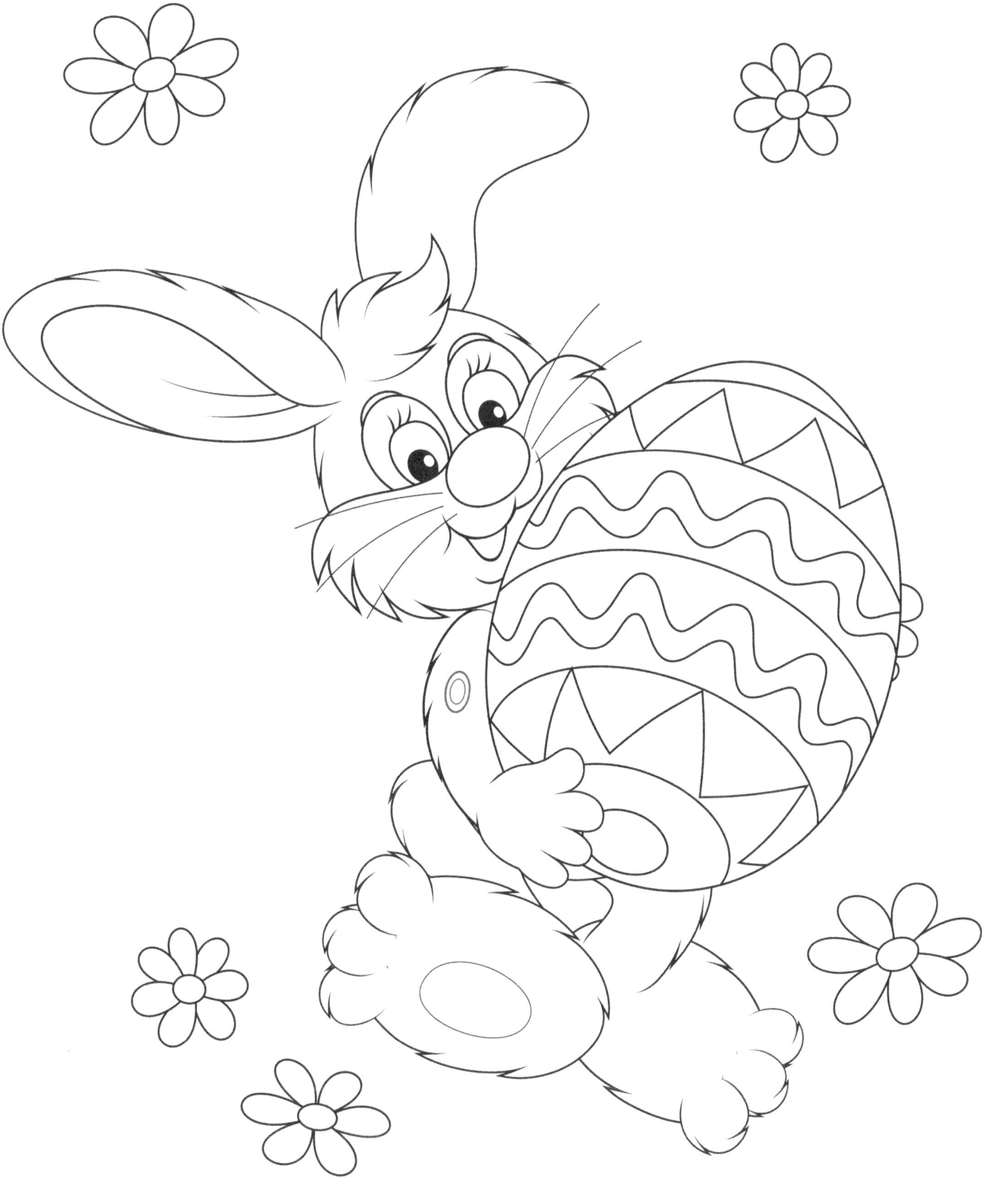

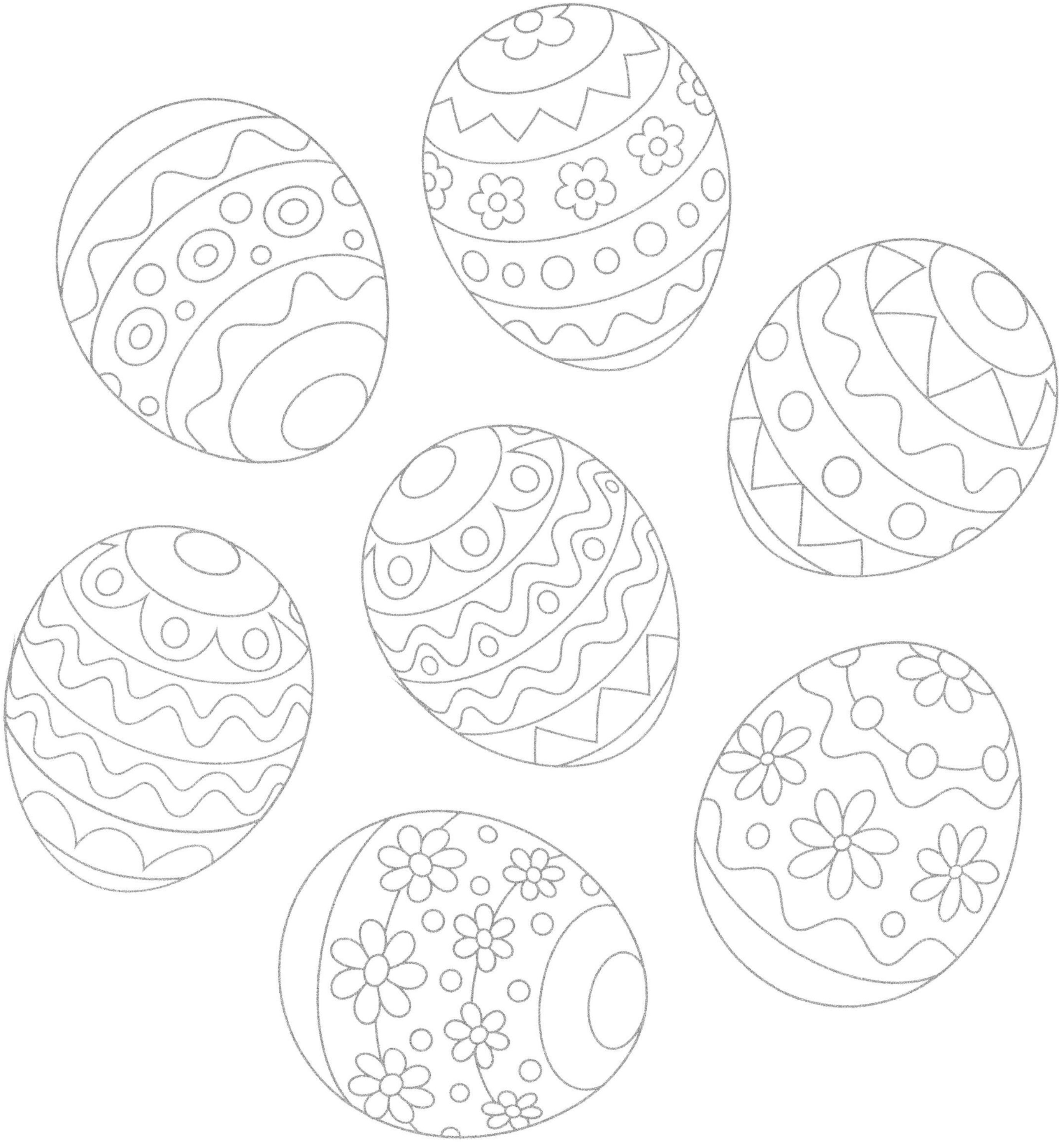

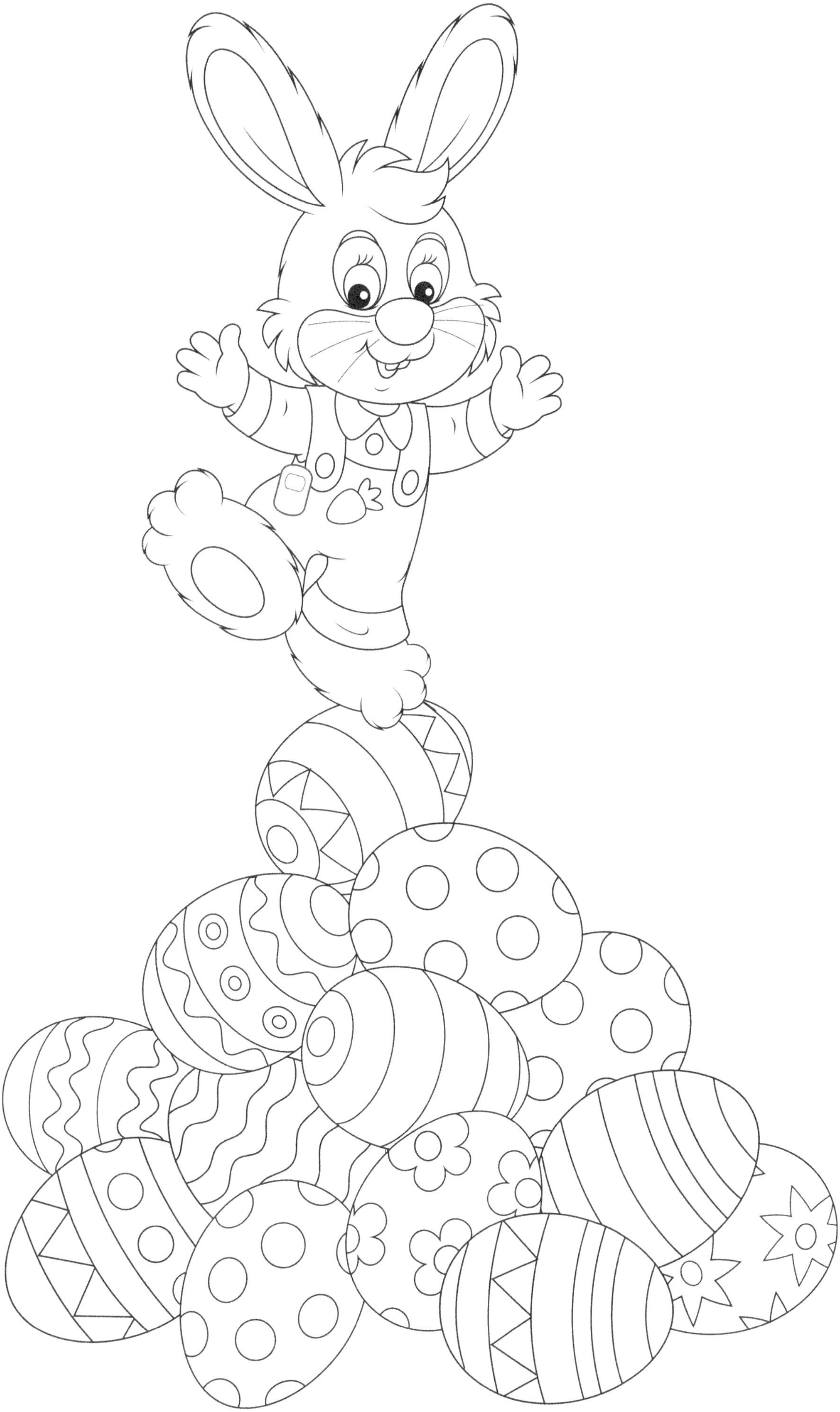

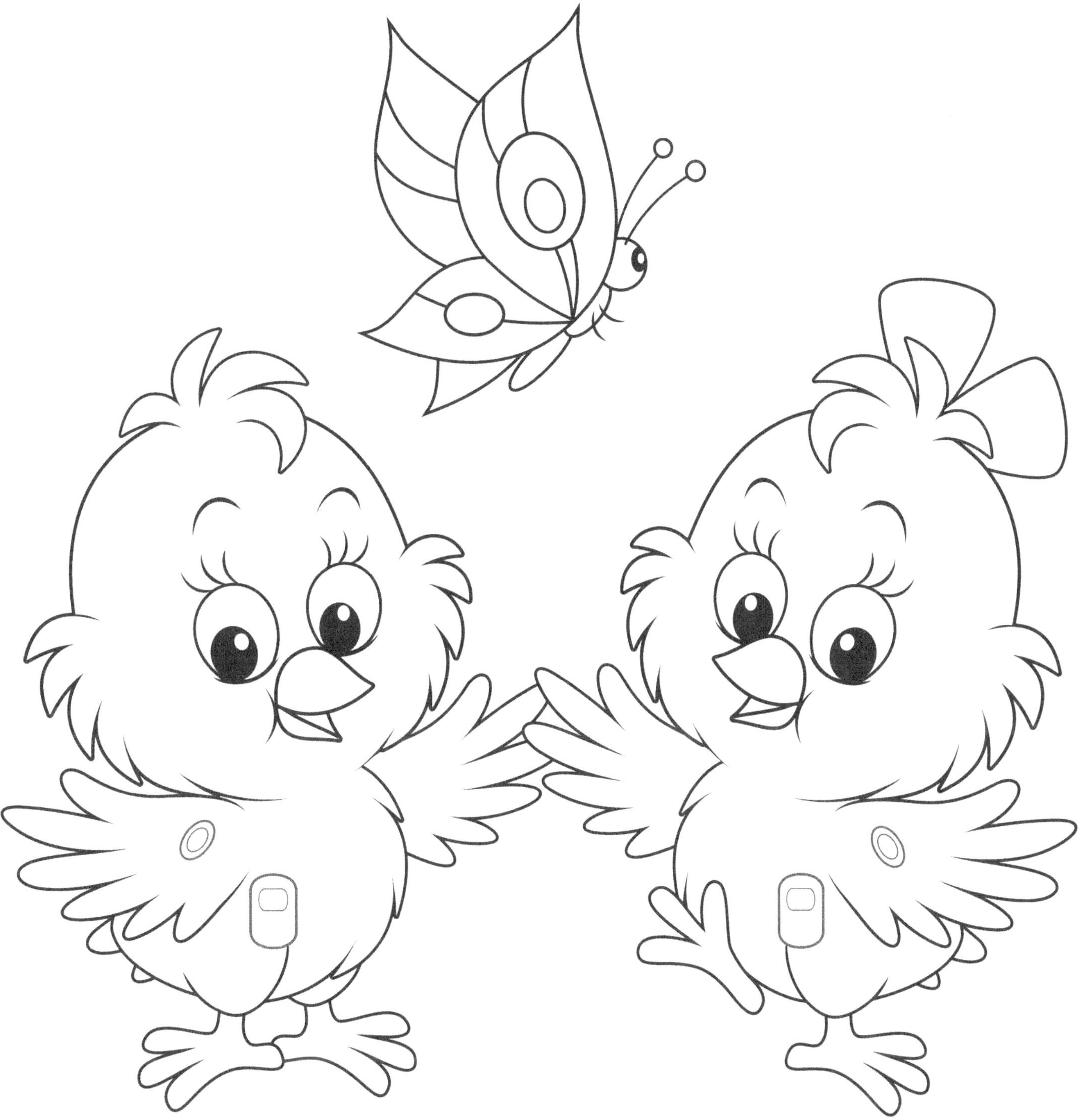

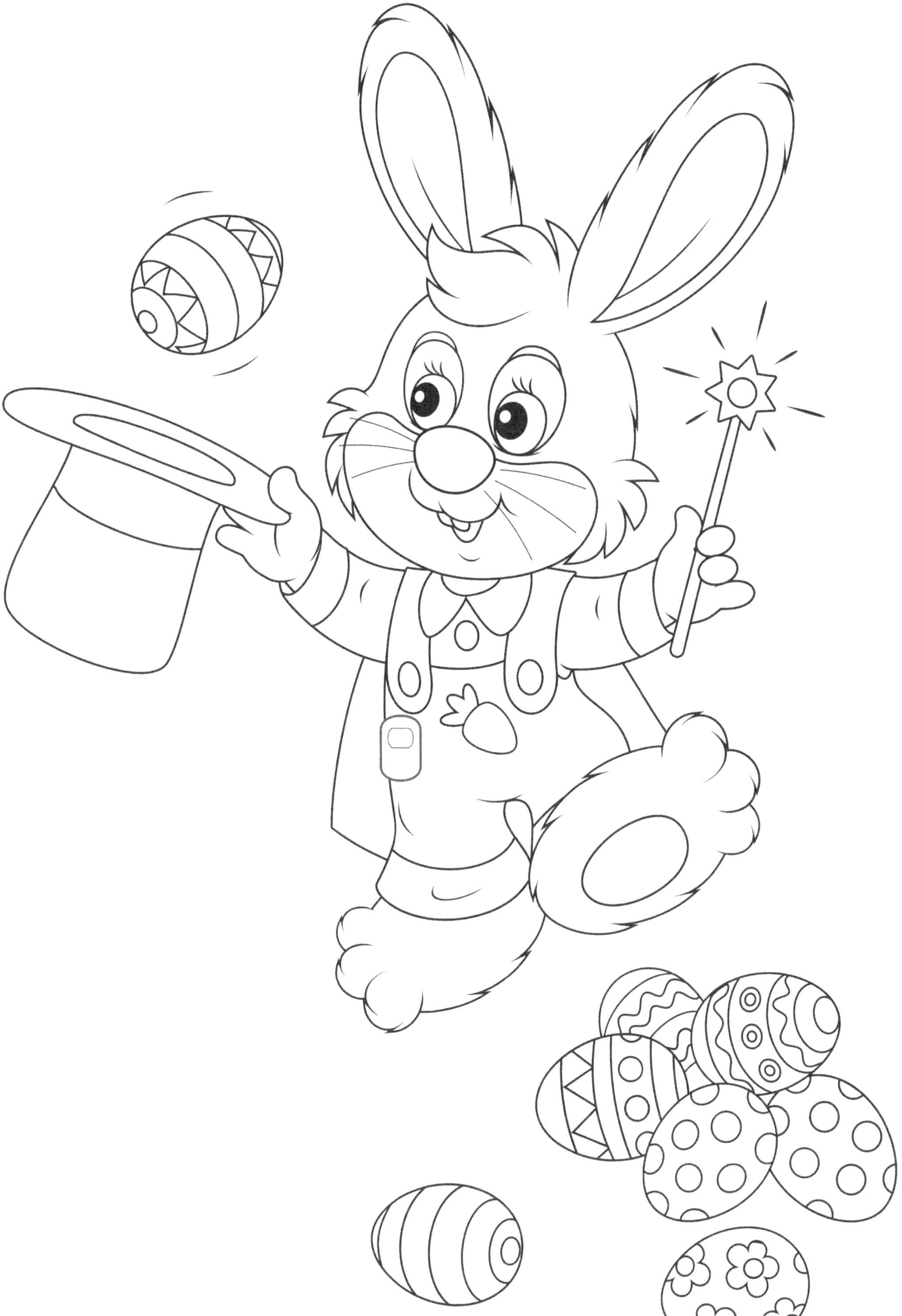

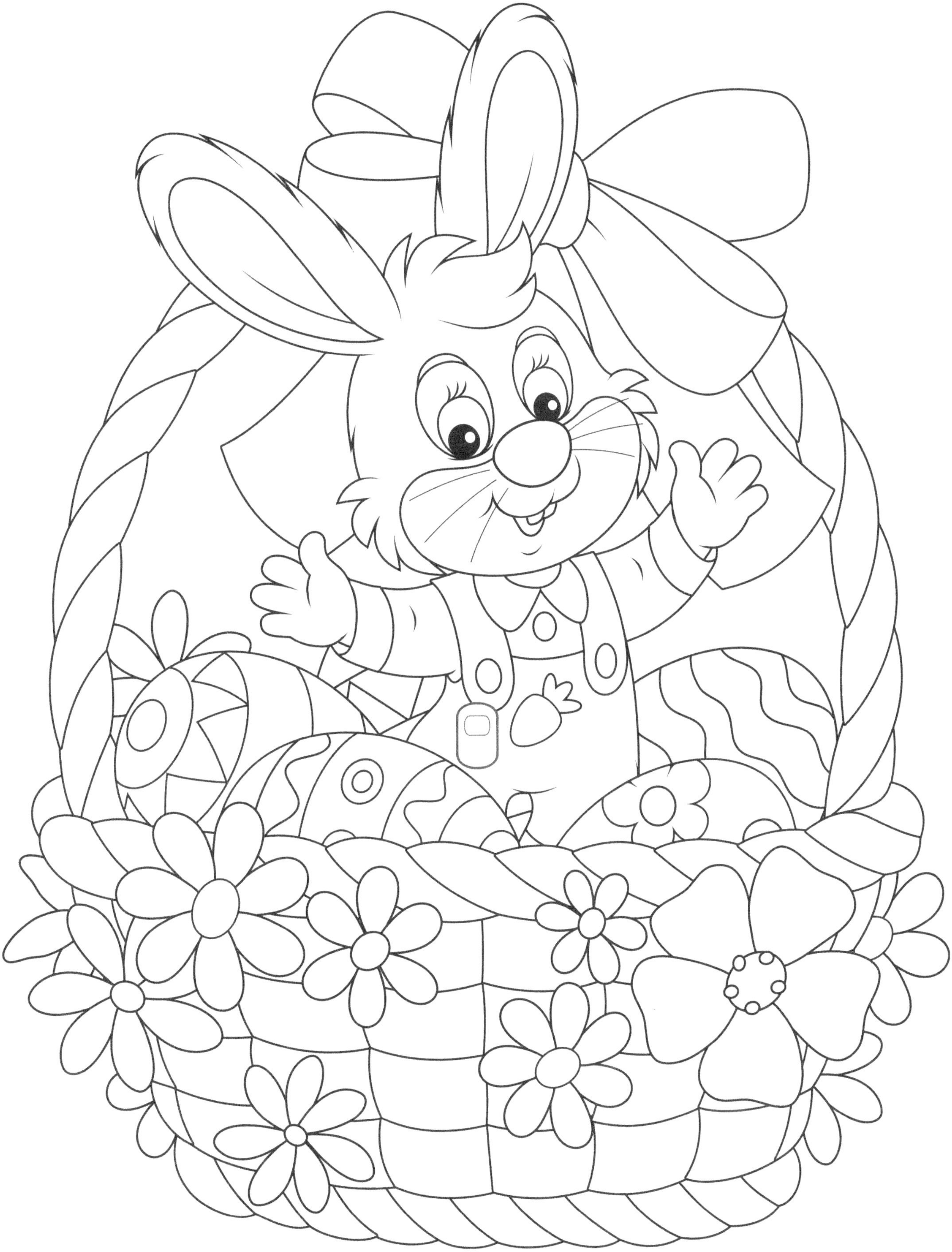

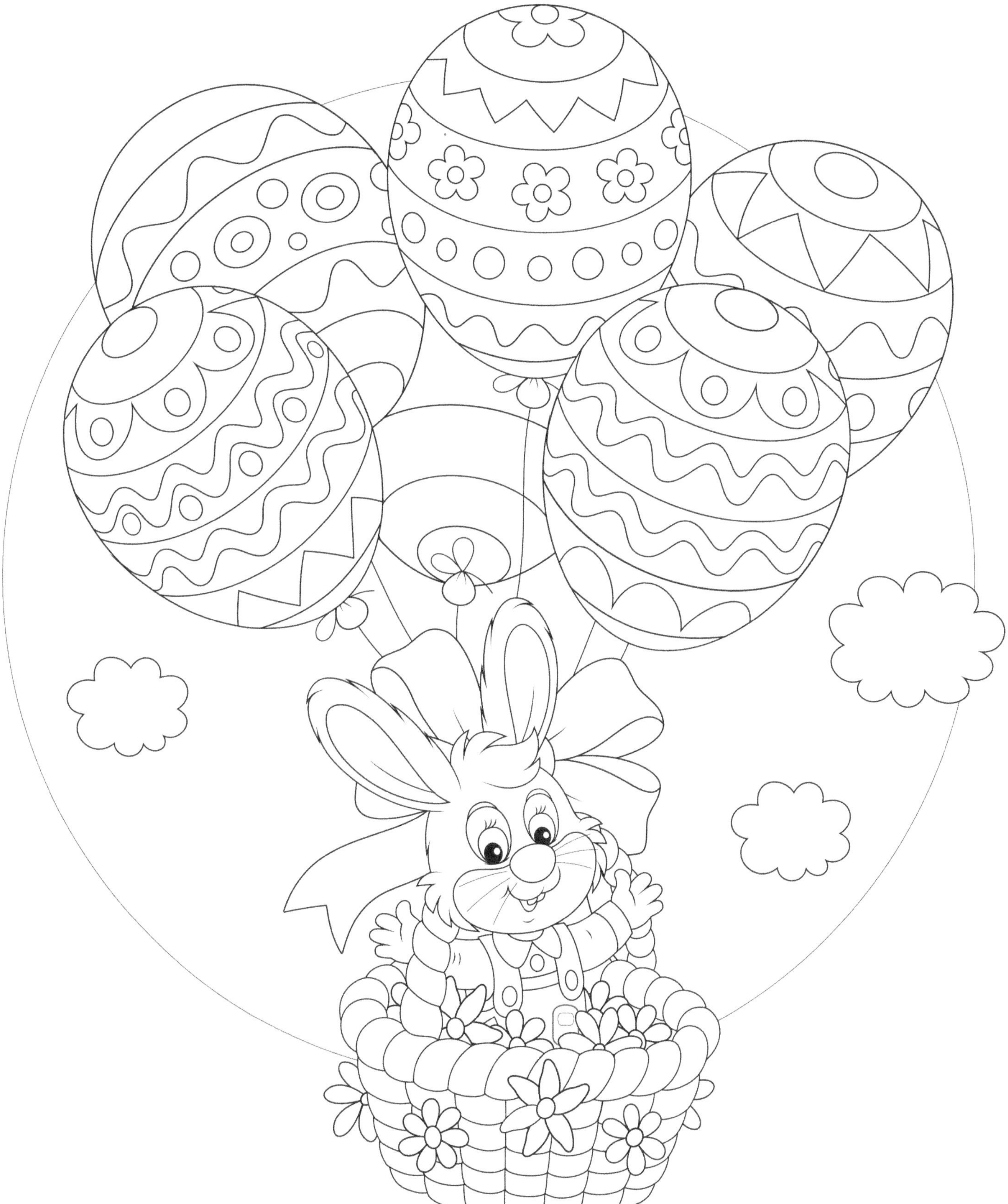

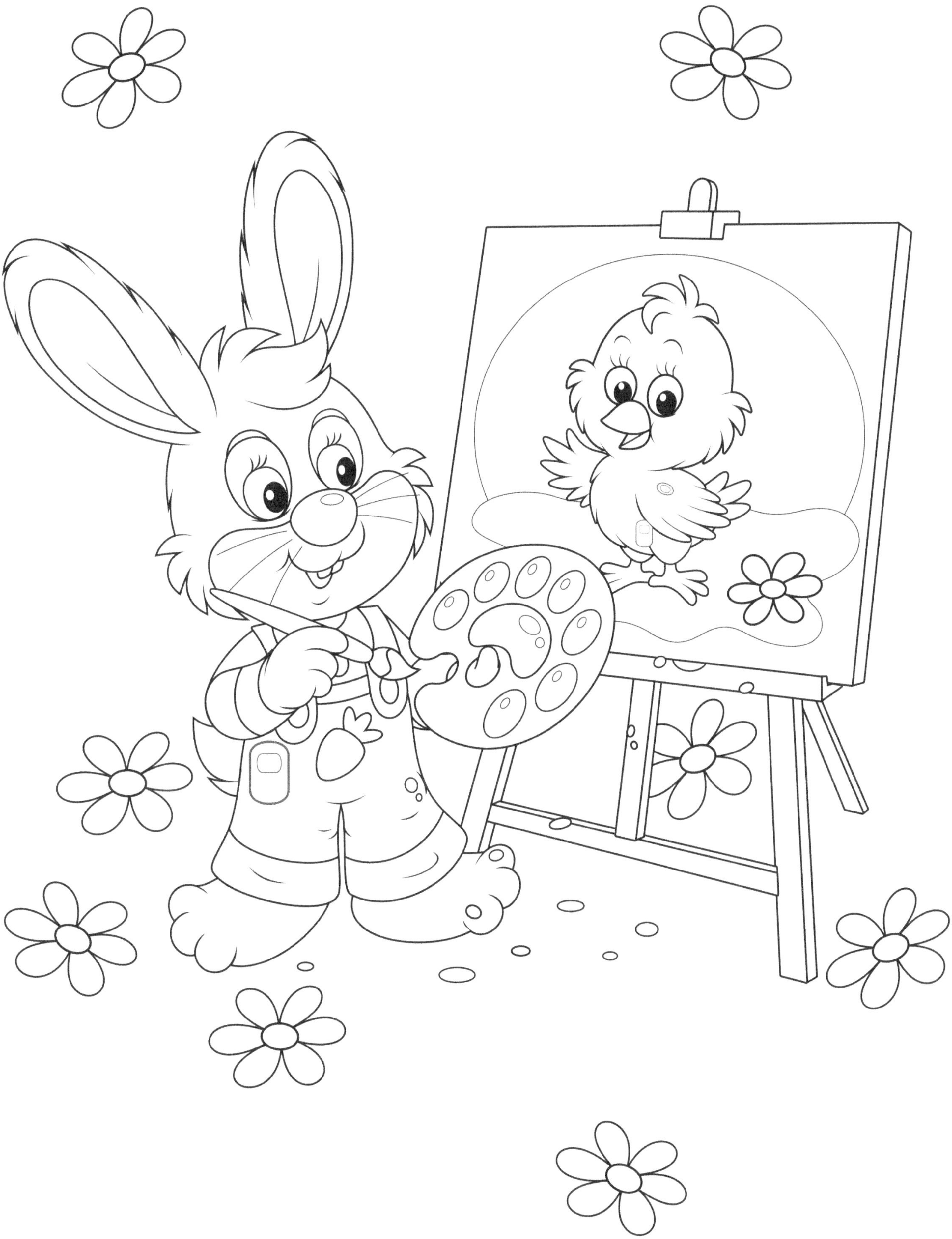

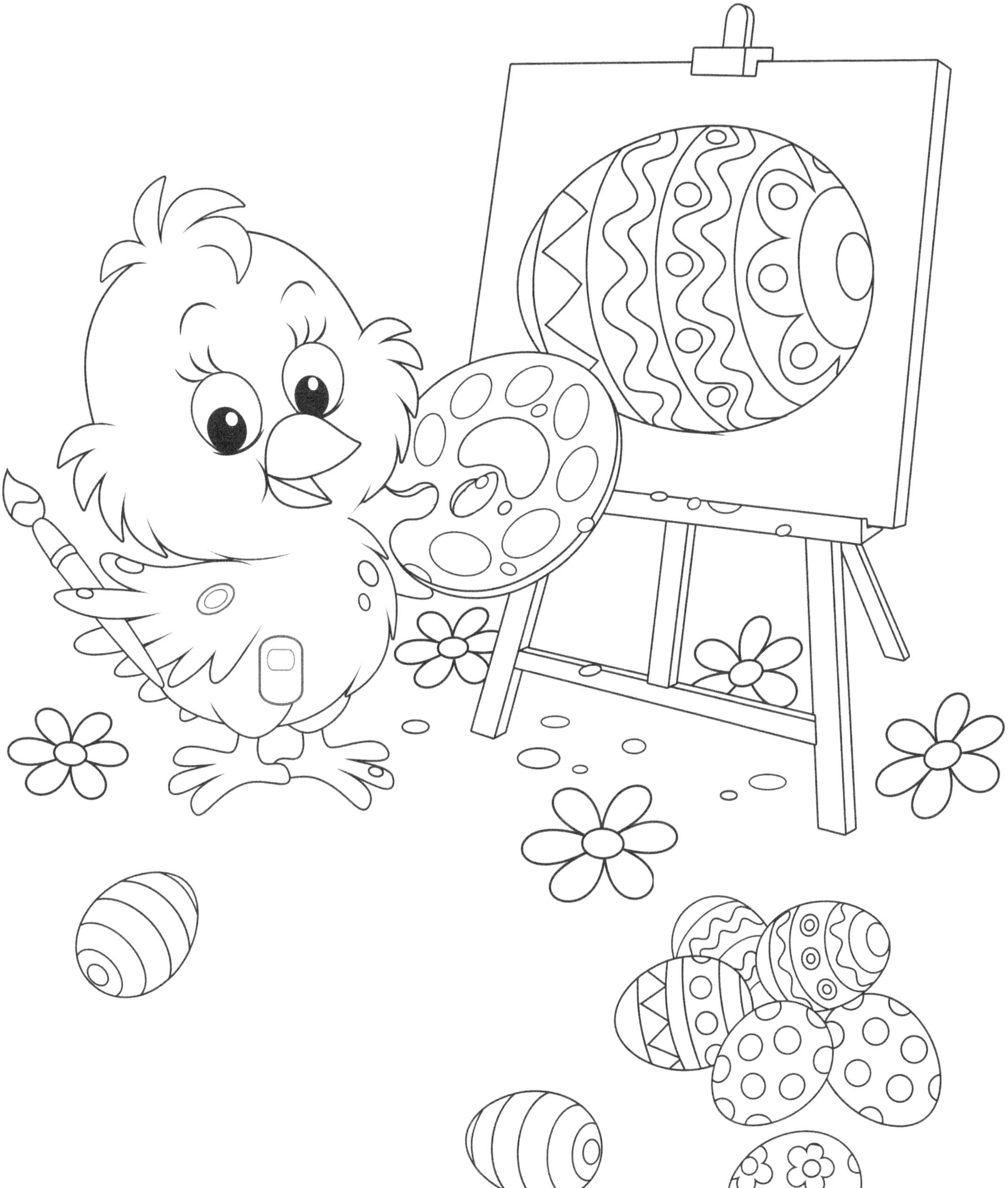

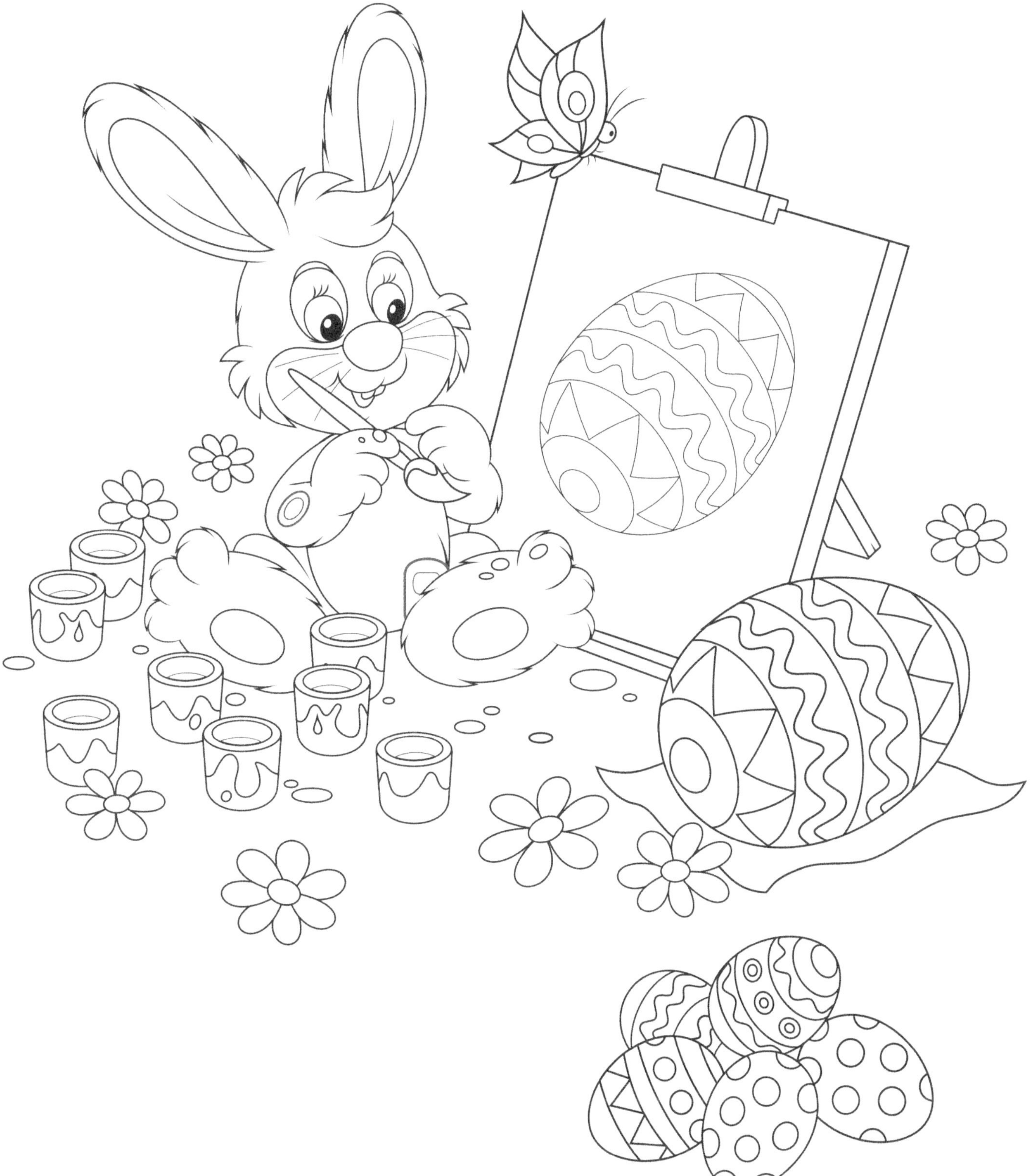

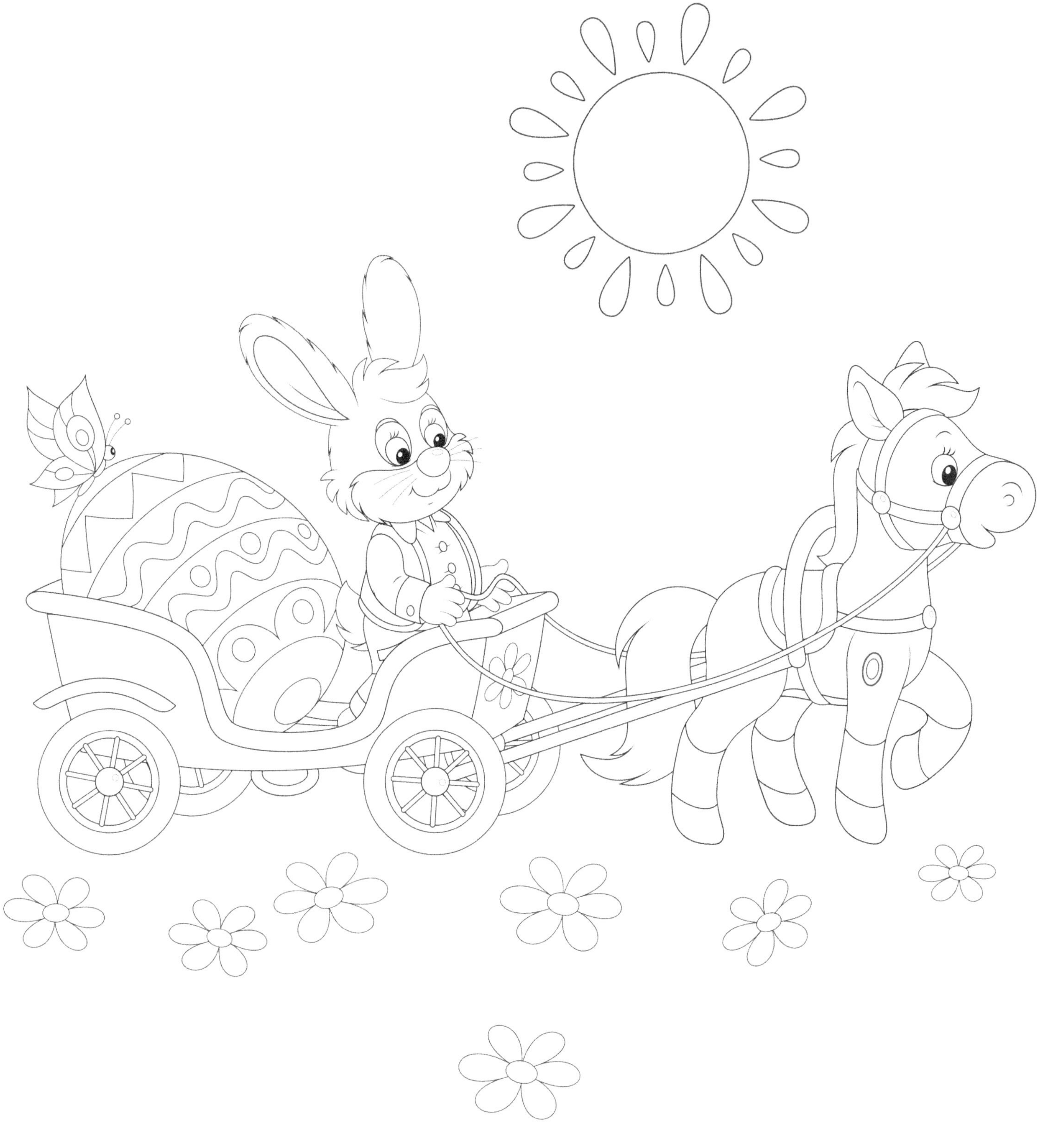

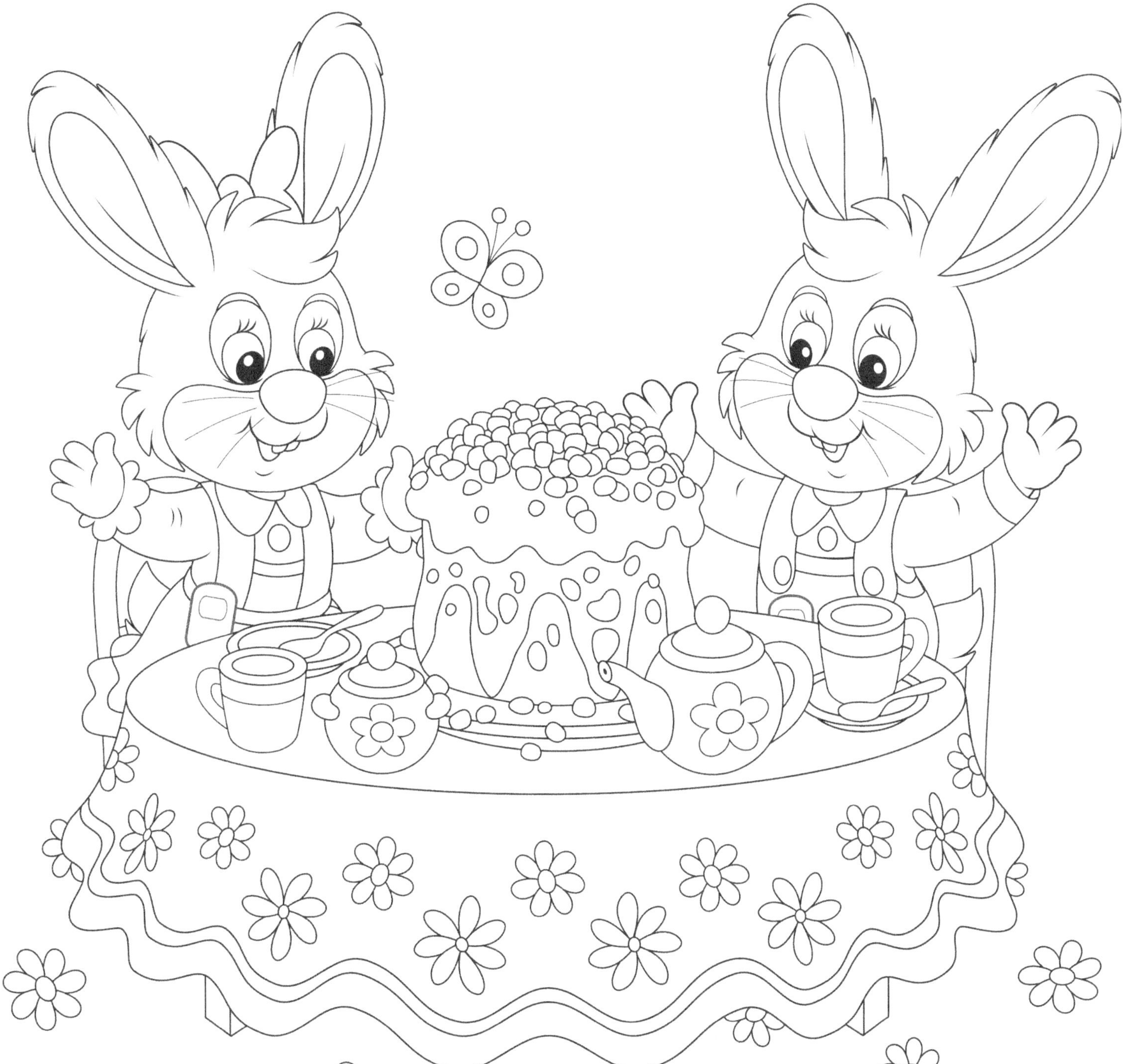

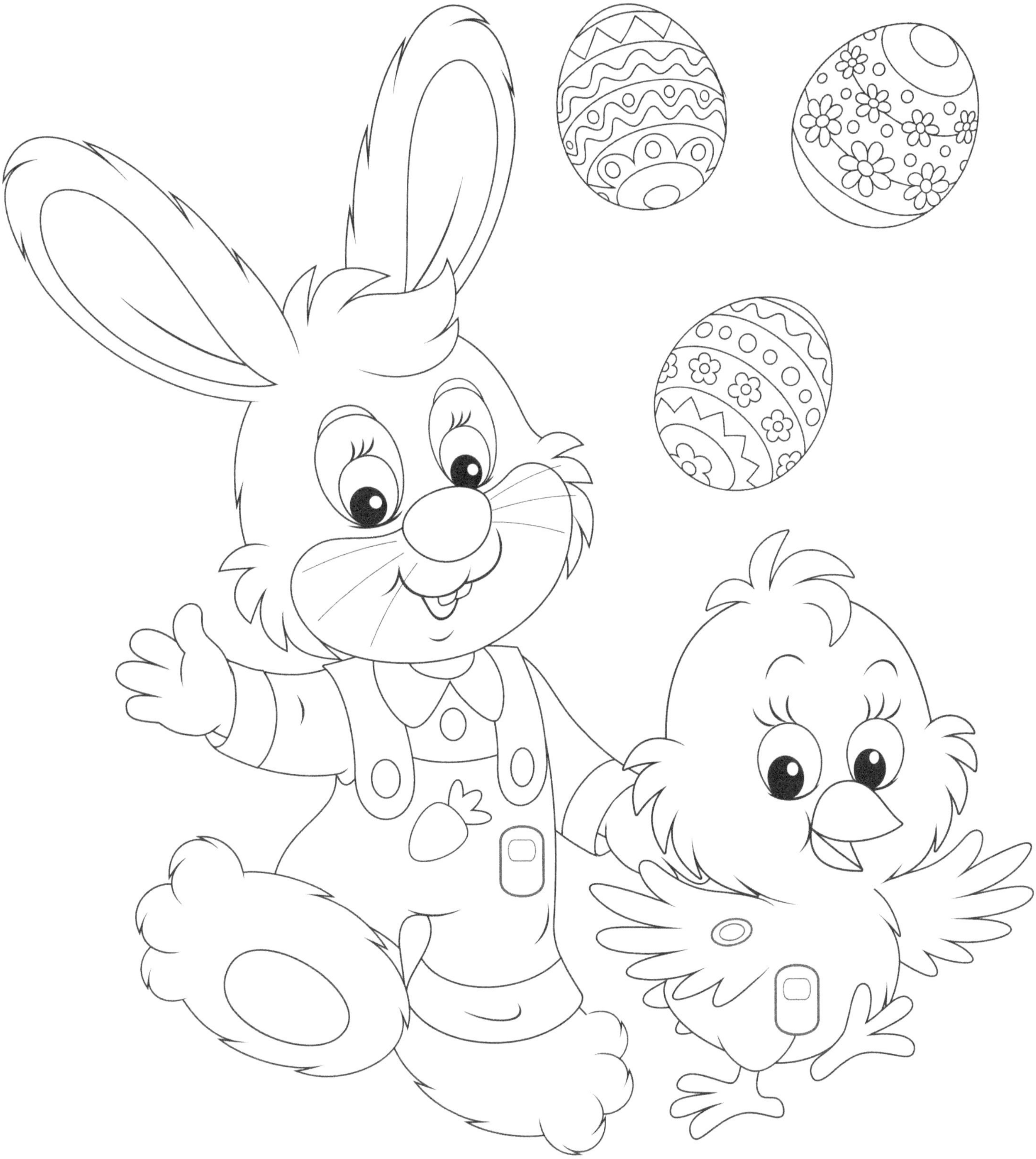

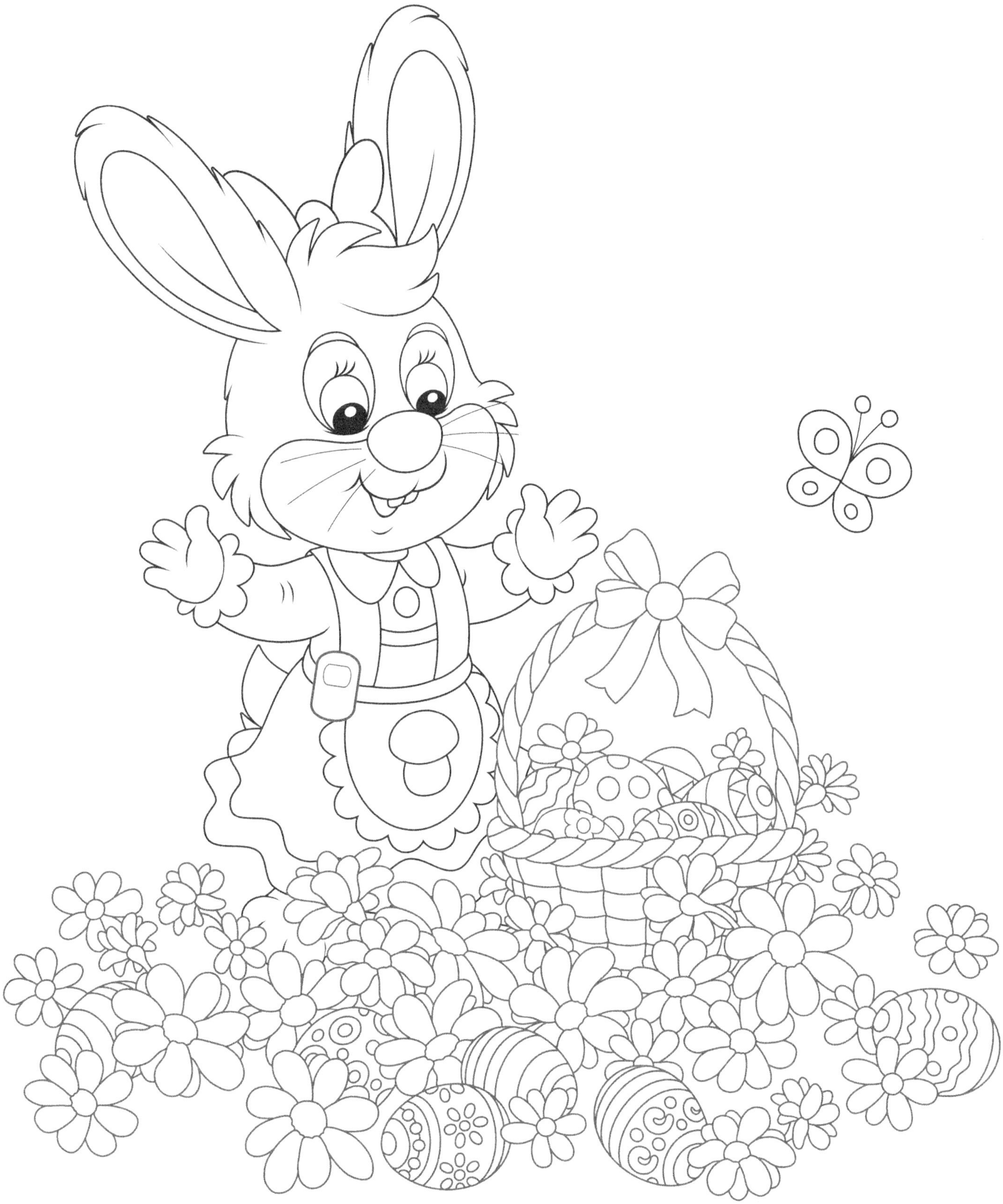

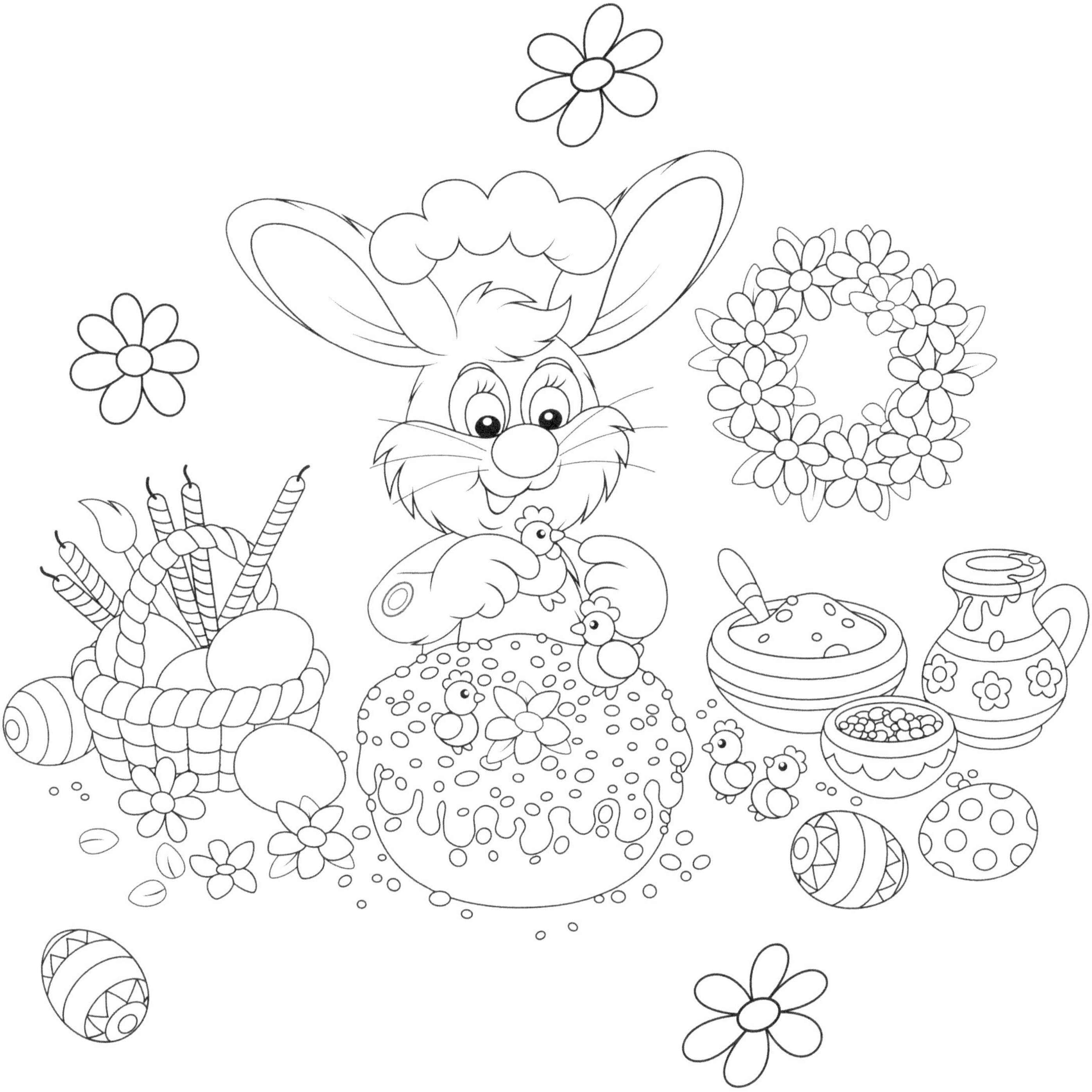

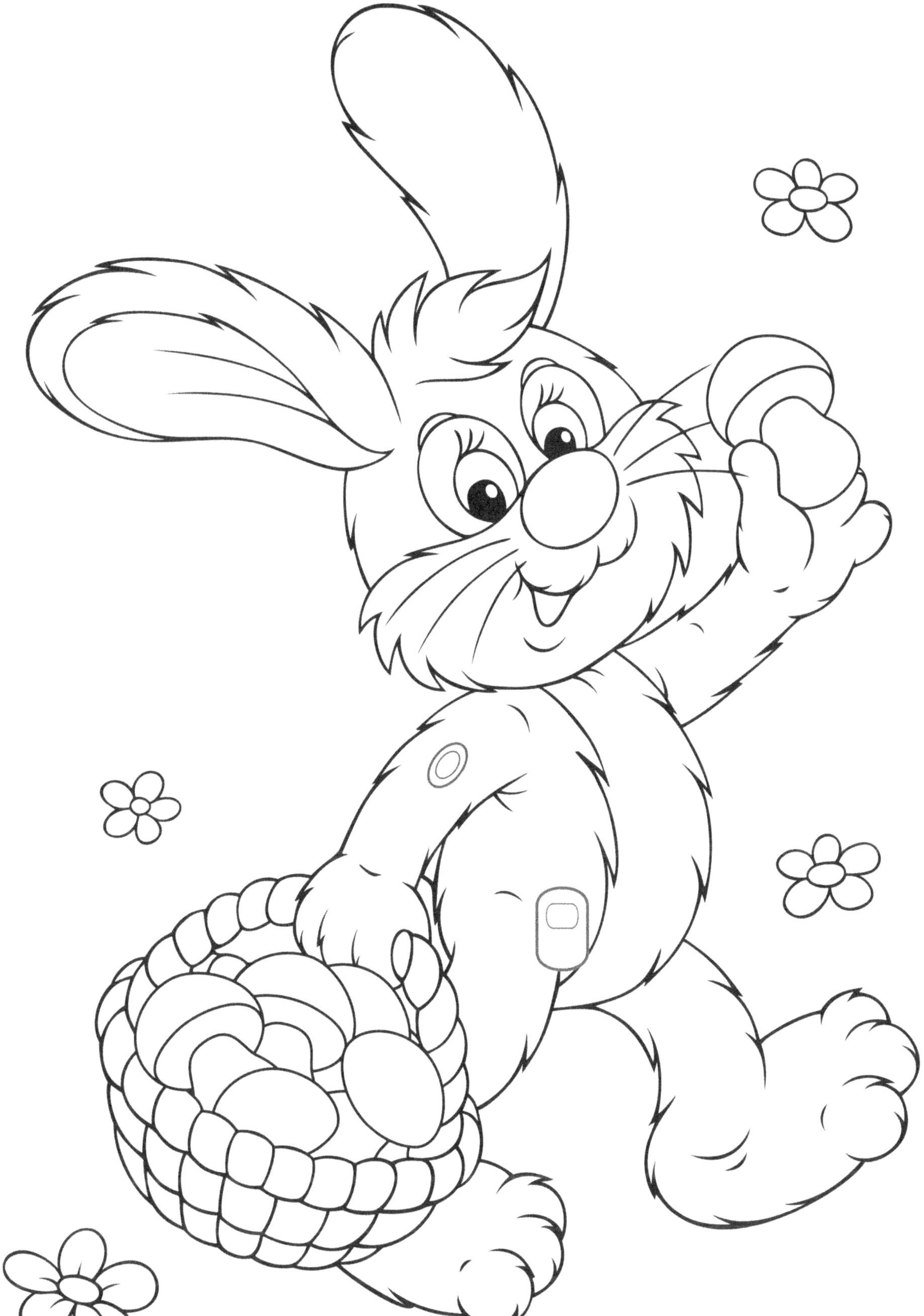

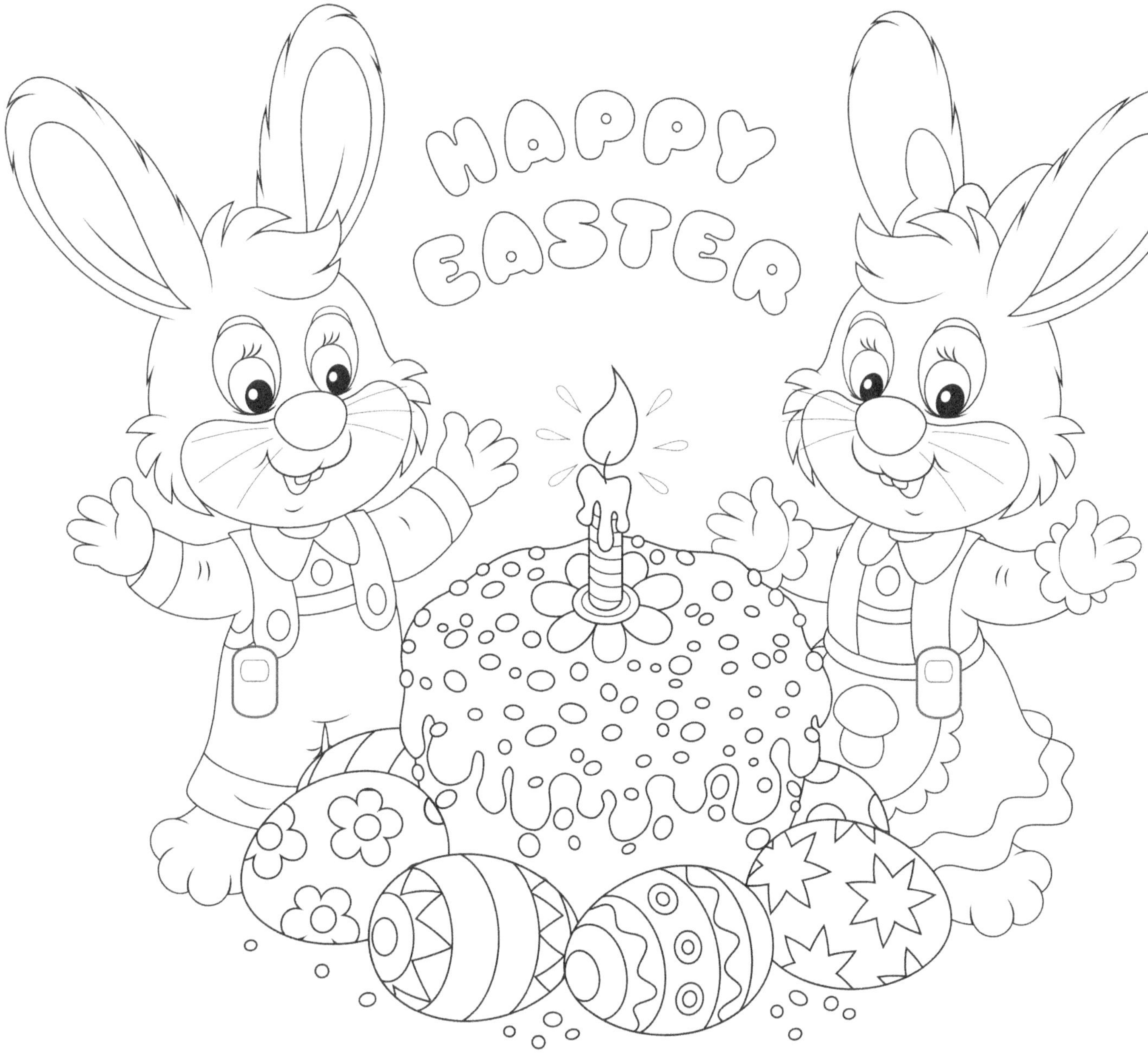
HAPPY
EASTER

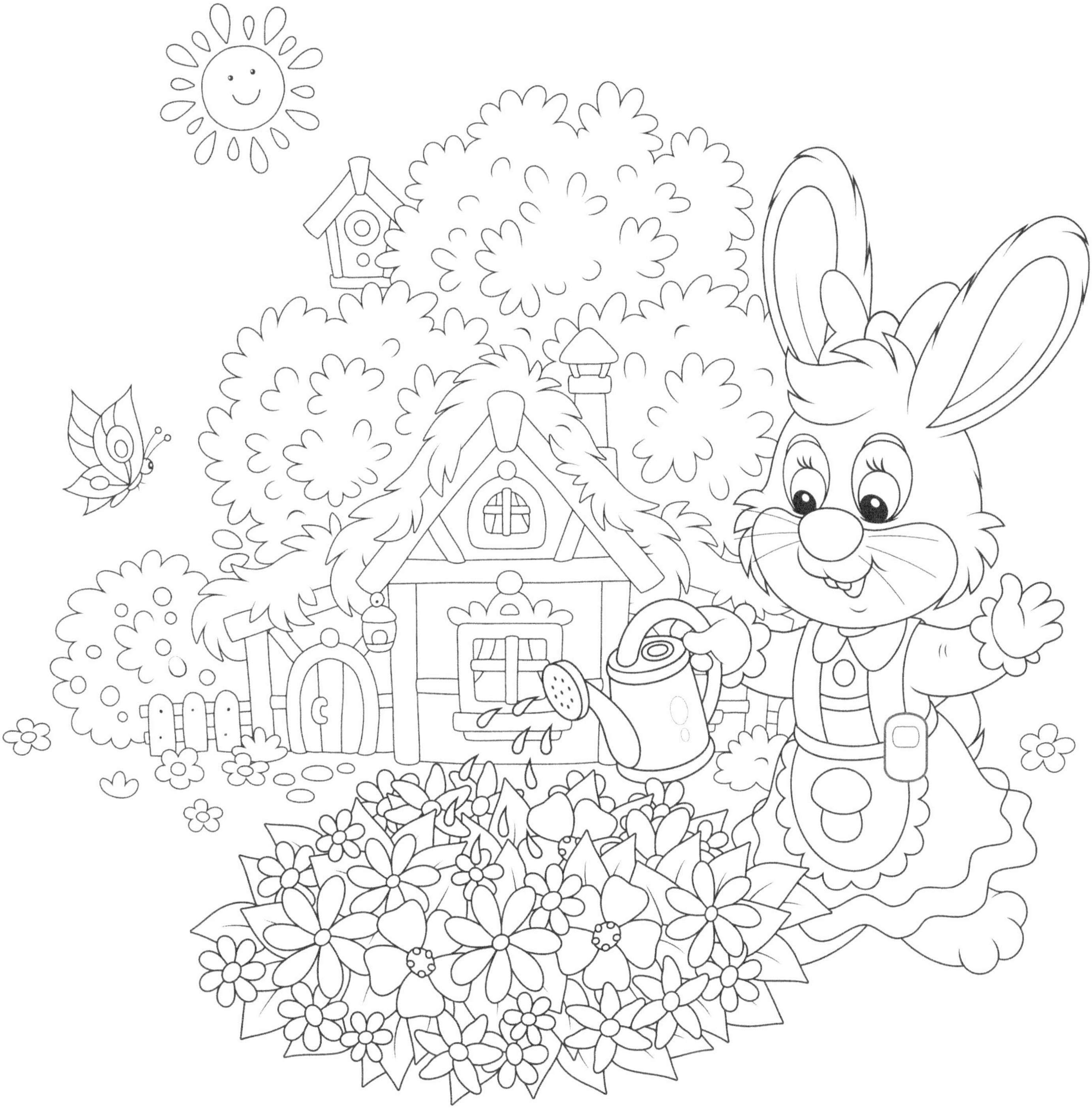

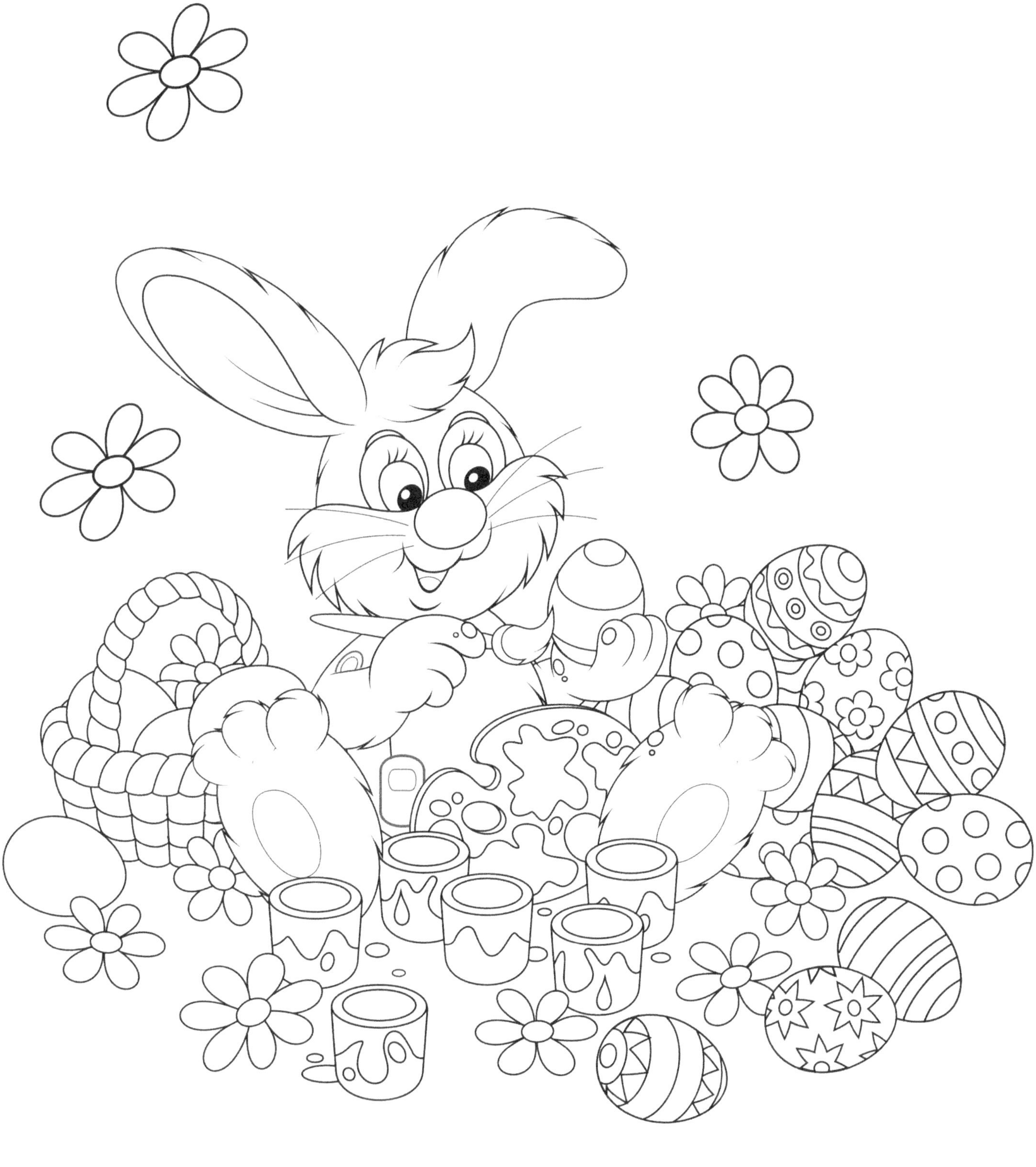

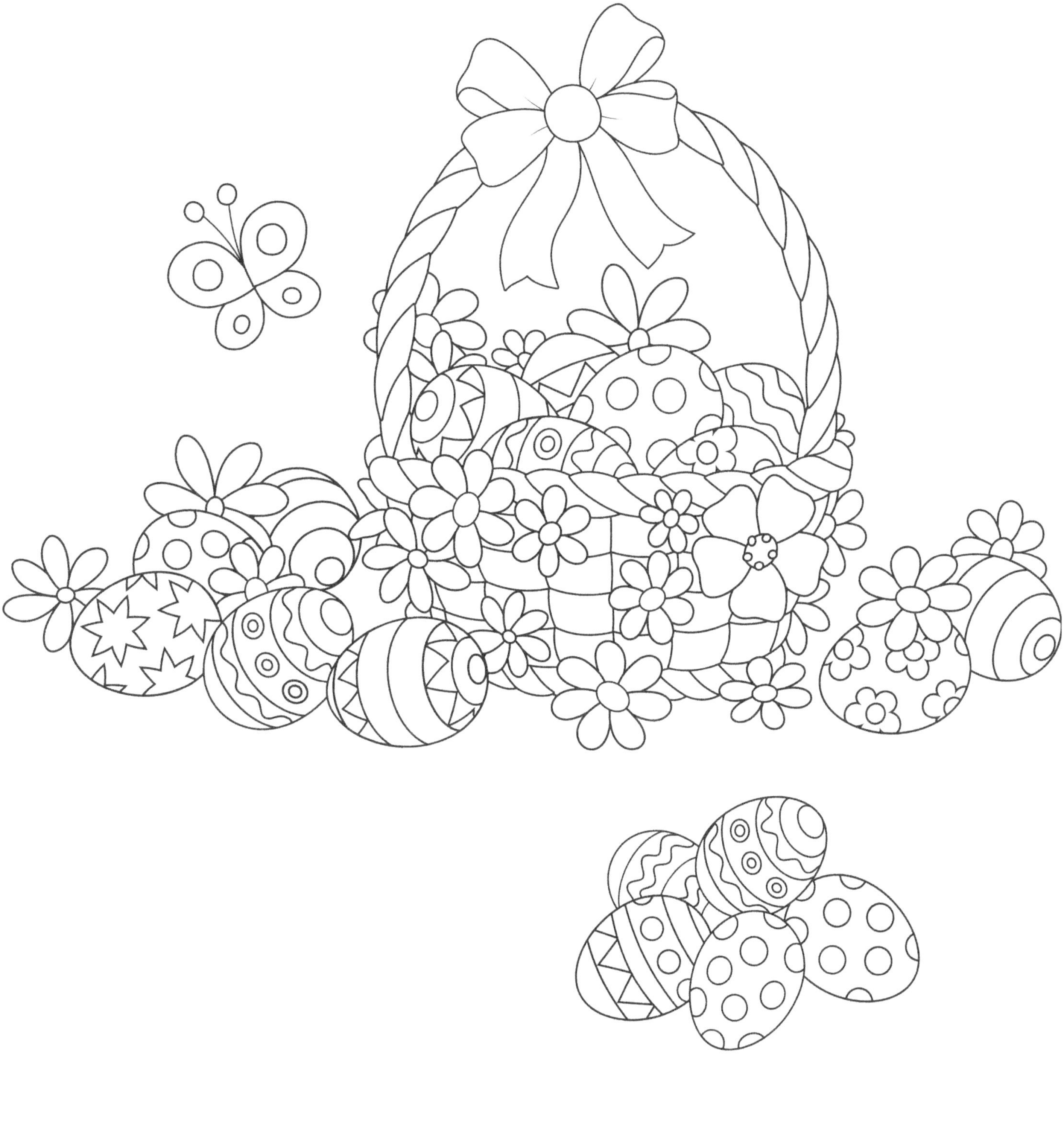

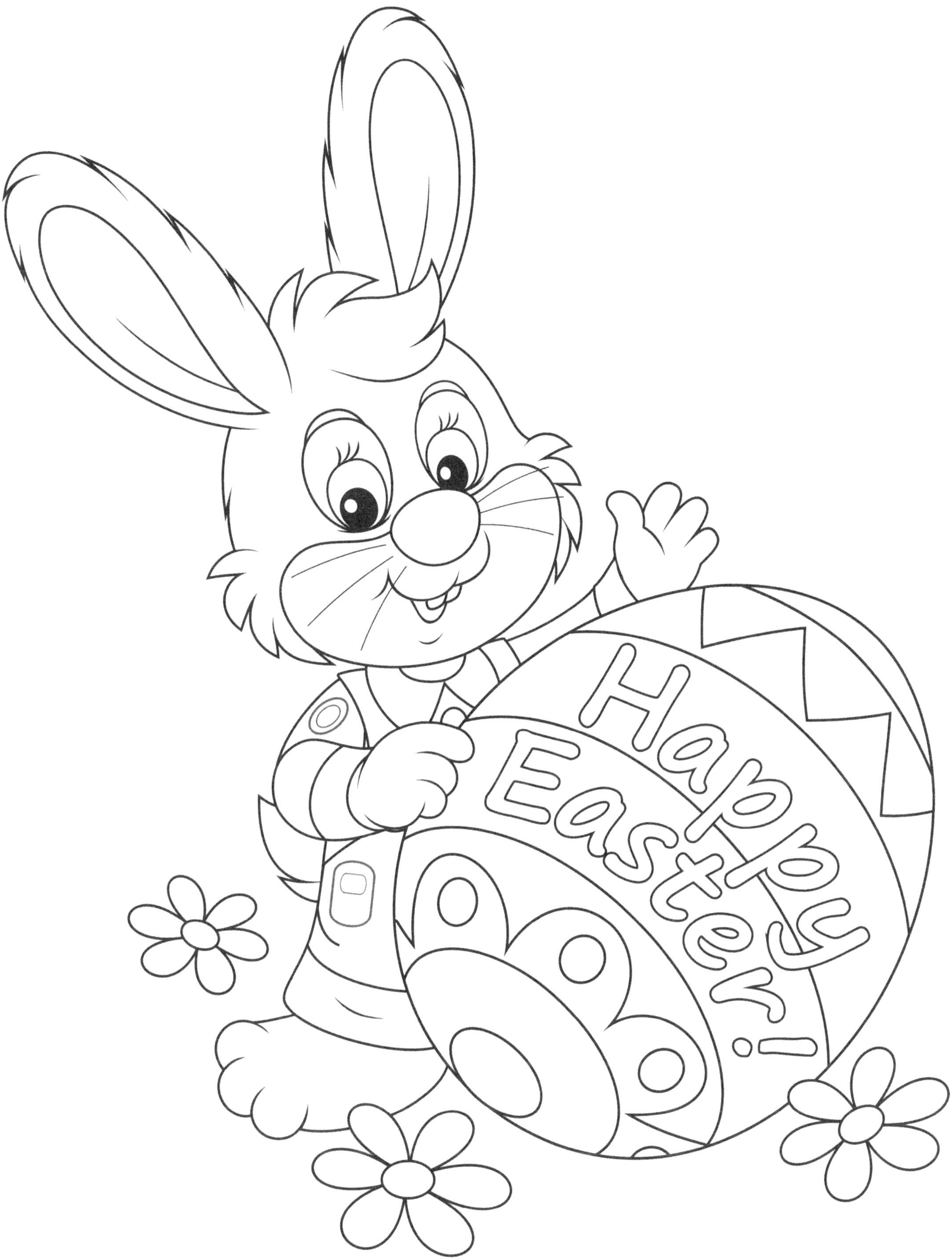
Happy Easter!

www.ingramcontent.com/pod-product-compliance
Lightning Source LLC
Chambersburg PA
CBHW081426280526
45788CB00009B/3238
* 9 7 8 1 0 9 0 5 1 3 2 0 5 *